NEW ZEALAND
SONGBIRDS

Text by Brian Gill
Drawings by Juliet Hawkins
Sound Recordings by Les McPherson

GODWIT

Published by Godwit Press Limited
P. O. Box 4325
Auckland 1

First published 1994

© 1994 Brian Gill (text)
        Juliet Hawkins (illustrations)
        Leslie McPherson (recordings)

ISBN 0 908877 40 4 (book)
     0 908877 41 2 (cassette)
     0 908877 39 0 (book & cassette pack)

Cover photograph by Geoff Moon
Printed in Singapore

Contents

Introduction

1. Brown Kiwi
2. Pied Stilt
3. Red-billed Gull
4. New Zealand Pigeon
5. Shining Cuckoo
6. Morepork
7. New Zealand Kingfisher
8. Skylark
9. Hedge Sparrow
10. Blackbird
11. Song Thrush
12. Grey Warbler
13. Fantail
14. Silvereye
15. Bellbird
16. Tui
17. Yellowhammer
18. Chaffinch
19. Greenfinch
20. Goldfinch
21. House Sparrow
22. Starling
23. Common Myna
24. Kokako
25. Australian Magpie

Introduction

All over the world, people's lives are brightened up by the sounds of birds, and it would be a very quiet and dull place without birds. In New Zealand, where many of the native songbirds are now rare or extinct, the settled areas would be deathly quiet were it not for the sounds of the birds introduced by the European settlers.

Most species of birds utter a variety of 'calls', and some sing 'songs' as well, all of which are given in different contexts for different effects. Calls are typically short, simple and given by both sexes at any time of year. Calls may signal a change in the bird's activity, help to maintain contact between birds in a group or signal alarm. Most birds give alarm calls if startled and distress calls if injured, which are usually so urgent and piercing that they alert birds of all species to the danger and may lead to the mobbing of a predator by all the birds in the immediate vicinity. Young birds use begging calls to solicit food from their parents.

Songs are more elaborate and are often produced only by males during the breeding season. Songs are most highly developed in the 'songbirds' – the largest single group of birds and the commonest garden birds. All the birds in this book from the skylark onwards are songbirds in the strict sense. The songs that many male songbirds perform in the breeding season are thought to advertise to rival males the singer's claim to his breeding territory and also help to attract and retain a mate.

This compilation of bird songs gives some of the sounds of twenty-three of the birds most likely to be heard in or near New Zealand towns and cities. To these we have added the brown kiwi, because it is the national bird, and the kokako, because it has the most beautiful and haunting native bird song.

In this selection of recordings we cannot
demonstrate all the calls that a species of bird
produces, so be aware that you may hear many other
calls from a particular species. Note also that some of
the native birds, like bellbirds and grey warblers, have
regional song dialects – grey warblers in Auckland
may sound slightly but consistently different from those
in Christchurch, although the general characteristics
of the song are recognisable anywhere.

References

Buller, W. L. *A History of the Birds of New Zealand.*
Van Voorst, London, 1873.

Guthrie-Smith, H. *Birds of the Water, Wood and Waste.*
Whitcombe & Tombs, Wellington, 1910.

Thomson, G. M. *The Naturalisation of Animals and Plants in
New Zealand.* Cambridge University Press, Cambridge,
1922.

Oliver, W. R. B. *New Zealand Birds.* Fine Arts, Wellington,
1930.

Falla, R. A.; Sibson, R. B.; and Turbott, E. G. *A Field Guide
to the Birds of New Zealand and Outlying Islands.*
Collins, London, 1966.

1

BROWN KIWI
Apteryx australis

As a name and an image the kiwi is well known, but the birds themselves are rarely seen, partly because they are nocturnal and partly because in most areas they died out as their forest habitat was destroyed. Few New Zealanders know that there are three species of kiwi, differing in size and coloration. The commonest is the brown kiwi, which persists in suitable areas from Northland to Stewart Island.

Brown kiwis call at night and at dusk and dawn. The male lets forth a string of loud, shrill whistles, usually seven to twenty-three at a time. The female's call is a shorter, hoarser cry. The nostrils are at the end of the bill, and while probing in soil and leaf litter to locate prey, kiwis make loud snuffling noises as they expel air from their nostrils. Kiwis may hiss and growl when aggressive or alarmed.

A correspondent of Buller's, familiar with the country inland from Wanganui, wrote: 'There are great numbers [of brown kiwis] still to be found in this district. They go together in companies of from six to twelve, and make the country resound at night with their shrill cry.'

Recording: Male and female calling in captivity, South Island birds, Kumara, April 1983, just after dark.

PIED STILT (Poaka)

Himantopus himantopus

Among the wading birds of New Zealand, few are as unmistakable as the pied stilt. The bold plumage is black and white and the gaudy legs are reddish pink. The body is about the same size as a city pigeon's, but the bill and legs are extremely long and thin, and the feet trail well behind the tail during flight.

Pied stilts eat sub-surface invertebrates such as crustaceans and earthworms, which they seize at the edge of ponds, shallow lagoons and swamps, or on riverbeds, estuarine mudflats and flooded fields. Stilts are often in groups and may be seen on the shore or in larger parks and reserves in, or close to, towns.

Their loud yapping call is like the yelping of a puppy and is heard to greatest effect when the birds are alarmed or excited and take off in a group. At various times sections of the stilt population migrate around New Zealand (between north and south and between coast and inland) and the calls of migrating birds may be heard overhead at night.

Buller thought it '. . . a pretty sight to watch a flock of them on the edges of a lagoon, stalking about in the shallow water . . . and displaying their well-balanced bodies in a variety of artistic attitudes'.

Recording: Small group at Milford Lagoon, South Canterbury, October 1988, early afternoon.

RED-BILLED GULL (Tarapunga)

Larus novaehollandiae

This is the smaller of the two common gulls in New Zealand, and the one most likely to attend seaside picnics. It is uncommon away from the coast. Red-billed gulls feed in coastal waters, at estuaries and along the shore, taking crustaceans, marine worms and larvae. However, they have adapted to man's activities and now forage in large numbers at rubbish tips and sewage outfalls. They also follow the plough and search for earthworms on wet pastures and playing fields. They are therefore very much a bird of coastal towns and cities, where their various harsh screams are common and characteristic sounds.

'It is a bird of very lively habits . . . At one time you will meet with a flock of fifty or more in council assembled, fluttering their wings, chattering and screaming in a state of high excitement; at another you will observe them silently winnowing the air, turning and passing up and down at regular intervals, as they eagerly scan the surface of the water. Here you find them ranged apart along the smooth beach like scouts on a cricket-ground . . .' (Buller).

Recording: Flock squabbling over food, Oban, Stewart Island, December 1969, mid-afternoon.

NEW ZEALAND PIGEON
(Kereru)
Hemiphaga novaeseelandiae

The New Zealand pigeon belongs to a group of tree-dwelling fruit-eating pigeons widespread in tropical and subtropical regions of the Old World. With an average weight of about 600 grams, they are large among pigeons. The New Zealand species declined as European settlers cleared large tracts of forest, but it increased after restrictions on shooting and is now common in most parts of the country with forest remnants. New Zealand pigeons occur in the more wooded areas of towns and suburbs, and have adapted to feeding and nesting in exotic trees.

New Zealand pigeons are herbivorous, eating a wide range of fruits, leaves and flowers. They play a major role in the dispersal of many native trees (for example, miro, tawa, karaka) because the seeds pass undamaged through the pigeon's gut.

They have various soft calls – coos and grunts. In the bush their calls can sometimes sound like a group of people talking in the distance. New Zealand pigeons fly noisily, and their loud wing-beats are usually more noticeable than their calls.

'When not engaged in filling its capacious crop with fruit or berries, it generally reposes on a thick limb . . . but on the slightest alarm it stretches up its lustrous neck, and gently sways its head to and fro, uttering a scarcely audible coo, slowly repeated' (Buller).

Recording: Pair in captivity, National Wildlife Centre, Mount Bruce, August 1979, early afternoon. (Flooded stream in background.)

SHINING CUCKOO
(Pipiwharauroa)

Chrysococcyx lucidus

Shining cuckoos belong to a group called the 'glossy cuckoos' because they have iridescent plumage. The members of this group are the smallest of all cuckoos – about the size of house sparrows. Shining cuckoos are dark iridescent green above, and below they have dark bars running from side to side on a white background.

The shining cuckoo has one of New Zealand's most distinctive bird songs. It is loud, clear and simple. Most cuckoos around the world have simple calls, probably because they do not rear their own young. The song is innate in the young bird and cannot be learned or modified by contact with their biological parents. Shining cuckoos, unwittingly or otherwise, are ventriloquists.

'The first notes always sound a considerable distance away and the rest appear gradually to approach the listener until the bird may be discovered within a few feet of him' (Oliver).

Shining cuckoos spend only the spring and summer in New Zealand, where they lay their eggs in the nests of grey warblers. When the cuckoo hatches, it pushes any eggs or other nestlings out of the nest and is reared alone by the foster parents. In autumn shining cuckoos migrate to the Bismarck Archipelago and Solomon Islands, east of New Guinea.

Recording: Lake Waihola, Otago, February 1975, late afternoon. (Golden bell frogs and various birds in background.)

MOREPORK (Ruru)

Ninox novaeseelandiae

This is our common owl – nocturnal and therefore seldom seen, but often heard. Moreporks roost in trees by day, where they usually go unnoticed, and emerge at dusk and at night. The morepork is a forest bird but has adapted to modified habitats and now occurs in pine plantations and in some wooded parks and suburbs. Moreporks eat insects and small vertebrates such as mice and geckos. Their search for insects may bring them to lamp-posts and the like, where they swoop down on insects attracted to the light.

Moreporks have various calls, the typical one being the two-part call that gives the bird its names – *morepork* or *ru-ru*. There is also a loud, shrill, vibrating *cree-cree*. Moreporks call throughout the night but especially during the early evening. Calling by day is rare.

'I sent my native lad, Hemi Tapapa, up the tree to capture them (two morepork nestlings); and while he was so engaged, the parent birds came forth from their hiding-place, and darted at his face with a low growling note, making him yell with fear . . . Hemi's conscience was troubled; and as the shades of night were closing in upon us with the call of ''more pork!'' in every direction, he handed me the captives and hurried away . . .' (Buller).

Recording: Skinner Reserve, near Whangarei, September 1981, just after dark.

NEW ZEALAND KINGFISHER (Kotare)

Halcyon sancta

Kingfishers have enormous beaks, seemingly out of proportion to the size of the body and feet. The archetypal kingfisher of Europe lives along rivers and streams and dives into pools to catch fish. However, the New Zealand species is one of the forest kingfishers, a group that knows no such limitations. These birds occur very widely in New Zealand in towns, farmland and at the edge of the shore or bush. They eat any moving prey that they can overpower, such as cicadas, dragonflies, lizards, crabs and, occasionally, small birds.

The kingfisher's commonest call is a loud, clear, repetitive *kek, kek, kek, kek*. Pairs on territories give various loud calls (a repeated *kreel* or a harsh scream) as they display to one another or confront intruders.

The nest is a cavity at the end of a tunnel excavated in a rotten branch or clay bank. As the nestlings grow, the nest becomes dirty with excrement and uneaten food.

'The birds know neither how to keep a cleanly house or rear a mannerly family . . . the young birds quarrel without cessation from daylight to dark, hour by hour, girning like bad-tempered children, the squabble alternately dying to a drone and heightening to a twangling chorus of treble shrieks' (Guthrie-Smith).

Recording: Skinner Reserve, near Whangarei, September 1981, just after dawn. (Blackbird and other birds in background.)

SKYLARK
Alauda arvensis

In open country all over New Zealand, including the larger parks and playing fields in towns, may be heard the skylark. This bird usually sings on the wing – as it rises up in the sky, as it hovers with rapid wing-beats facing into the wind, or as it descends. The song is 'a torrent of trills and runs, fast, variable and sustained' (Falla, Sibson & Turbott). It can be heard in all months but least often in autumn.

Skylarks were introduced from Europe in large numbers between 1864 and 1879. As an antidote to the settlers' homesickness for the sounds of the British countryside, skylarks seemed to be much in demand. They were released in many areas and soon established throughout the country, only to become a pest of agriculture from their habit of uprooting the seedlings of crop plants. They seem to cause fewer problems for today's farmers.

Recording: Several birds singing in flight, Lake Ellesmere, November 1971, mid-afternoon.

HEDGE SPARROW (Dunnock)

Prunella modularis

This small brownish bird is similar to the female house sparrow but slimmer and with a sharper, more slender bill. It was brought from Britain and liberated many times around the country by acclimatisation societies between 1867 and 1882. There is doubt about some of the introductions because many at the time '. . . did not know a hedge-sparrow from a common sparrow . . . (and) no one is inclined to claim any credit for the latter' (Thomson).

Hedge sparrows are at home in orchards, scrub, farmland and gardens, where they usually stay close to cover. They are common garden birds in many New Zealand towns and cities but are inexplicably rare in Auckland. They lay bright-blue unspotted eggs in their cup-shaped nest. Hedge sparrows feed mostly on the ground, eating seeds and invertebrates (insects, spiders, etc.). They are very much the farmer's and gardener's 'friend'.

From April to January, hedge sparrows sing, usually from a prominent perch. The song is fast, shrill and jerky, and has been aptly expressed by W. Garstang as *weeso, sissy-weeso, sissy-weeso, sissy-wee.*

Recording: Christchurch, August 1984, mid-afternoon.

BLACKBIRD
Turdus merula

This superb songster is common in virtually every New Zealand garden or park, and is one of the few introduced birds that thrives deep in the native bush. The male (illustrated) has glossy black plumage and a yellow to orange bill. Females and immatures are brown with some dark speckling on the breast, and they have dull-coloured beaks.

Blackbirds are a mixed blessing to orchardists, as they eat soft fruits as well as harmful insects. They were introduced in the 1860s. Lady Barker, travelling from Melbourne to New Zealand in 1865, wrote: 'Ill as I was, I remember being roused to something like a flicker of animation, when I was shown an exceedingly seedy and shabby-looking blackbird . . . bought in Melbourne as a great bargain . . .' (*Station Life in New Zealand*, 1870).

The blackbird's beautiful song is given only by the male in the breeding season from July to January. It is loud, clear and melodious. When disturbed, blackbirds give a loud, urgent alarm call.

Recording: Christchurch, November 1984, early evening.

SONG THRUSH
Turdus philomelos

This close relative of the blackbird is equally at home in our gardens, parks and settled countryside. It is similar in shape and movements to the blackbird, though a little smaller. Both sexes are brown, with pale but boldly dark-spotted underparts. Female blackbirds are sometimes confused with song thrushes, but the latter have much paler underparts.

The diet of the two species is similar, but song thrushes appear to take more garden snails, which they carry to a suitable rock or other hard surface – their 'anvil' – and batter them, scattering the broken shells nearby.

Song thrushes were first established here in the 1860s, having been brought from Britain. Their song has the same clear melodious beauty as the blackbird's, and is heard mainly between May and December. It is more shrill and less mellow than the blackbird's song, and the thrush usually repeats each phrase of the song several times.

Recording: Christchurch, December 1984, early evening.

GREY WARBLER (Riroriro)

Gerygone igata

The grey warbler is, with the rifleman, our smallest bird. It weighs about 6.5 grams, only a third the weight of a mouse. Grey warblers have dull-grey plumage, but the eye is bright red in adults and brown in young birds.

Grey warblers occur throughout New Zealand wherever there are trees and shrubs. They are common in towns and suburbs but, being so small and drab, are much more often heard than seen.

The song is a beautiful wavering trill given only by males. They sing throughout the year but most often in spring when they nest. There is a Maori saying: 'I hea koe i te tangihanga o te riroriro?' ('Where were you when the grey warbler sang?'), which shames a lazy person who has cultivated no food.

Breeding males may perch on a prominent twig and gradually rotate as they broadcast their song. This was nicely described by Guthrie-Smith, who thought the warbler's song 'rather a cricket's cry than a bird's': 'Presently, from some manuka thicket, a sombre plumaged little bird will emerge, light on some topmost twig, and pour forth to three-quarters of the globe – for in his ecstasy he nearly sings a circle – this faint sweet trill that heralds fuller spring.'

Grey warblers eat insects and other arthropods. They are unusual among New Zealand songbirds in building an enclosed, pear-shaped nest with a small entrance at one side.

Recording: Spencerville Plantation, near Christchurch, September 1971, morning.

FANTAIL (Piwakawaka)

Rhipidura fuliginosa

Acrobatic flying is the fantail's speciality. The long tail trails behind during flight but may be spread like a fan periodically as the bird hops between perches. Fantails catch flying insects while they themselves are on the wing. The bill is short and broad as an adaptation to this way of feeding. Fantails appear to be friendly or inquisitive towards humans, but in reality they have a habit of following the progress of any large animal through their home range to catch the insects that are disturbed.

Fantails are common throughout New Zealand. The nest is a tightly woven cup raised high above the twigs to which it is attached. Up to four young may be raised at one time.

The fantail's song is a rambling chatter. There is also a single call that birds utter repeatedly to maintain contact.

'Long may the pied fantail thrive and prosper . . . for without it our woods would lack one of their prettiest attractions, and our fauna its gentlest representative' (Buller).

Recording: Franz Josef, December 1956. (Other birds in background.)

SILVEREYE (Tauhou)

Zosterops lateralis

In winter, flocks of silvereyes (also called waxeyes or white-eyes) visit gardens all over New Zealand in search of insects, berries and nectar, which they drink from flowers. At this time they give contact calls that seem to us sad and plaintive. During the breeding season (spring and summer) flocking ceases and breeding birds are heard singing. There are at least two songs, one quite vigorous, and the other more subdued. 'During the breeding-season the male indulges in a low musical strain of exquisite sweetness, but very subdued, as if singing to himself or performing for the exclusive benefit of his partner' (Buller).

When silvereye pairs settle onto territories to breed, they build a dainty nest that tends to hang like a hammock between its points of attachment to surrounding twigs. 'The two or three delicate eggs of pale blue hang in the frailest looking fairy basket imaginable, a diaphanous cradle, woven on to frond or branchlet, and stirred by every breath of wind' (Guthrie-Smith).

In 1856, large numbers of silvereyes arrived in New Zealand, presumably from Australia, and the species soon spread throughout the country. The Maori name means 'stranger'. The Europeans at first called the silvereye the 'blight-bird' because it ate aphids, which were causing problems for apple growers. Silvereyes benefit the gardener by eating damaging insects, but they also peck soft-skinned fruits like grapes and figs.

Recording: Song, Greymouth, December 1956. (Other birds in background.)

BELLBIRD (Korimako)
Anthornis melanura

The bellbird is one of New Zealand's three species of honeyeaters – a family of birds best represented in Australia and New Guinea. Honeyeaters have brush-tipped tongues, an adaptation for the effective supping of nectar from flowers. The tongue can be extended into a flower about ten times per second, and nectar is drawn by capillary action onto the frayed portions of the tongue. Honeyeaters pollinate many of the flowers at which they feed, and, by eating berries, they effectively spread seeds.

Bellbirds form long-lasting pair-bonds, and breeding pairs establish home ranges. However, these often overlap, and many bellbirds may leave their home ranges to gather to feed at large flowering trees. In these sociable situations there is much calling, displaying and chasing.

Bellbirds are excellent songsters. Three distinct male songs and a female song have been identified. These comprise pure-frequency bell-like notes, quiet notes, and often mixed-frequency 'chonks', 'clonks', 'gurgles' and 'jarrs'. Neighbouring males may sing in unison. A mated male and female, or neighbouring birds, may countersing. Young bellbirds learn the songs that they hear in their first year, and because the birds do not move great distances, song dialects occur from place to place.

Recording: Taupo, September 1956. (Kingfisher in background.)

TUI (Parson Bird)

Prosthemadera novaeseelandiae

The tui is a honeyeater, like the bellbird, and they share many habits and characteristics. Both are widely distributed in New Zealand and may visit suburban gardens to feed in suitable trees.

The tui's song contains pure bell-like notes and a range of other sounds — 'clonks', 'rattles', 'wheezes', 'chuckles', 'clicks' and 'squeaks'. It is more variable than the bellbird's. Some of the tui's high-frequency notes are beyond our range of hearing. Tuis are mimics and are reported to have mimicked human whistles, the squeals of pigs, and other birds – including bellbirds. The songs of the two honeyeaters are easily confused; tuis rarely give bell-like notes if bellbirds are absent from the area.

Guthrie-Smith heard a tui, which he presumed to be the female, singing on the nest. 'We were close to her, yet she sang as if her song could have no ending, as if the world was too full of the ecstasy of life for wrong and rapine to exist . . . Much of the tui's singing we cannot hear, the notes too high, I suppose, for our human ears, for I have often watched the bird's throat from but a few yards' distance swelling with song entirely inaudible.'

Recording: Kapiti Island, October 1956.

YELLOWHAMMER
Emberiza citrinella

Yellowhammers were widely introduced from Britain between 1862 and 1871 by acclimatisation societies in Auckland, Nelson, Canterbury and Otago. They soon spread to all suitable areas and became a pest where grass was being sown for pasture and in grain-growing districts. Yellowhammers are sparrow-sized and brown in colour, apart from some bright yellow on the head and underparts, especially on the male during the breeding season.

Yellowhammers eat the seeds of grasses and low herbs, but they also eat large numbers of insects and spiders. As with many herbivorous birds, they bring insects to their nestlings, which require high-quality protein for growth. Yellowhammers prefer open areas like farmland, especially where it is bordered by rougher ground. In winter they form large flocks that move about to forage on seeds. It is then that yellowhammers are most likely to be seen in town – in parks and on playing fields.

The yellowhammer's song, heard mainly in spring and summer, is a distinctive chattering one, given rapidly except for the last segment, which is paused. The song sounds rather like 'a little bit of bread and no *cheese*'.

Recording: Mapara, near Te Kuiti, January 1988, early evening. (Sheep and running water in background.)

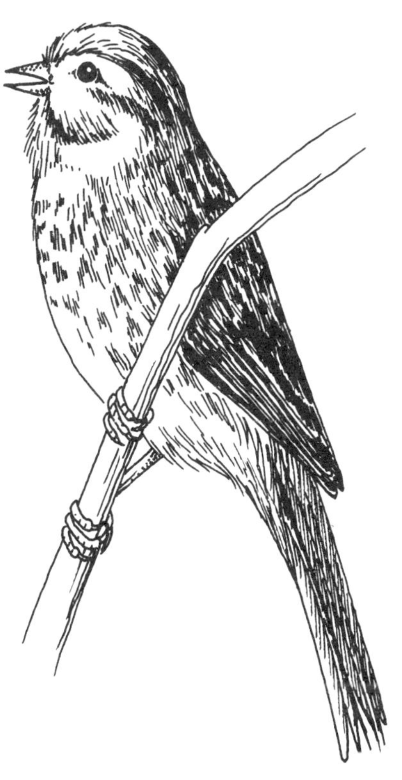

CHAFFINCH
Fringilla coelebs

This is another common European songbird that was successfully established in New Zealand in the 1860s and 1870s by the efforts of private individuals and the acclimatisation societies. Chaffinches are sparrow-sized. The female is drab, very like a house sparrow, but the male (illustrated) has slaty-blue plumage on the top of his head and the back of his neck, and a bright pinkish-brown face and underparts.

Chaffinches eat small seeds and insects. They are one of the most widely distributed birds of New Zealand, at home in native forest, pine plantations, farmland, parks and gardens. In town they will take food from bird tables. The cup-shaped nest is usually ornamented on the outside with pieces of lichen.

There are various short calls, but the song, given by males during the breeding season, is fast and loud – a series of short notes ending with a flourish, which was rendered by W. Garstang as *chip chip chip tell tell tell cherry-erry-erry tissi cheweeo.*

Recording: Lake Rotoiti, Nelson Lakes National Park, December 1969, before dawn. (Other birds in background.)

GREENFINCH
Carduelis chloris

The greenfinch was introduced from Britain in the 1860s and became a pest by damaging orchard fruit and eating grain. Many small introduced birds became such serious pests of agriculture that organised poisoning took place and bounties were paid for their skins and eggs. Happily this seems to be a lesser problem today than it was last century.

The greenfinch is about the size of a house sparrow but has a more massive bill. The male is a dull greenish colour. The female is browner and is easily confused with a house sparrow, but both she and the male have a touch of yellow on the wings and tail.

Greenfinches are common throughout New Zealand in farming areas and pine plantations. They are also seen in towns, especially in parks and larger gardens. The diet of greenfinches is mainly seeds, and the birds often occur together in large feeding flocks, especially in winter.

There is a twittering song, but perhaps more noticeable is the persistent call – a drawn-out *tswee* – given by males in spring and summer.

Recording: Song, Rough Island, Nelson, November 1969, late morning.

GOLDFINCH
Carduelis carduelis

Smaller and daintier than a house sparrow, the goldfinch is unmistakable with its bright-red face and intense yellow patches on the wings. The sexes are alike.

Goldfinches were liberated about the country many times between the 1860s and 1880s, and are now common in settled areas. They have similar seed-eating, winter-flocking behaviour to the greenfinch. Goldfinches often enter gardens in search of seeding plants. Being small and light, they are able to climb slender weeds like thistles to get at the seed heads. If the foliage bends, they quite happily hang upside down as they feed.

The flight of goldfinches is light and undulating. They have a musical, bubbling, liquid, twittering song, which they give from a perch or on the wing, in spring and summer.

Recording: Christchurch, November 1969, afternoon.

HOUSE SPARROW

Passer domesticus

The members of the sparrow family probably originated in tropical Africa. One species – the house sparrow – has become so adapted to living near human habitations that it rarely breeds away from towns and settlements. Having spread with people to virtually every major settled region – except China and Japan – the house sparrow is probably the world's most widely distributed land bird.

House sparrows were introduced to New Zealand by acclimatisation societies in the 1860s. One of the main reasons for their introduction was the hope that they would eat caterpillars and other pests that were threatening agriculture in the young colony. However, sparrows soon became pests in their own right and today they continue to damage cereal crops and cause nuisance in towns.

House sparrows are highly sociable, often feeding by day and roosting at night in large flocks. They do not have a complicated, melodious song, but instead give various chirps and chattering calls. One call sounds a little like *cheer-up.*

T. B. Hill, writing in 1916 of his success in acclimatising house sparrows some fifty years before in the Auckland suburb of Freemans Bay, stated: 'So many of us then were not yet acclimatised ourselves that when we woke in the morning hearing the little ''cheer-up, cheer-up'', it made us fancy we were back in the old country again' (Thomson).

Recording: Christchurch, October 1969, afternoon.

STARLING

Sturnus vulgaris

The starling, originally a European bird, has been spread by humans to North America, South Africa and Australasia, and is now one of the world's commonest birds.

Starlings feed mainly on the ground, particularly on short pasture, where they probe in search of ground-dwelling invertebrates. They have been encouraged in New Zealand in recent years because they eat grass grubs and other pasture pests. On the ground starlings walk, whereas many other common garden birds hop. For much of the year starlings feed together in large flocks and roost communally at night in large trees.

The starling's song can be heard all year, and consists of a variety of throaty, warbling, clicking, gurgling sounds. It is frequently given from a prominent perch, often while the wings are held out a little from the body and flapped. The starling is a mimic both of other birds and of other sounds.

'These birds are abundant in most parts of the country, and in favourite spots, where they congregate in numbers, the noise they make when roosting can be heard, literally for miles' (Thomson).

Recording: Christchurch, March 1981, mid-morning. (Vehicle traffic and dogs in background.)

COMMON MYNA

Acridotheres tristis

The common myna is a close relative of the starling and has a similar shape and the same jerky walk.

It was widely introduced in the 1870s but persisted only in the northern half of the North Island, where it is now one of the commonest birds of towns and settled districts. Its native home is a vast area from Afghanistan across India to south-west China. Apart from New Zealand, the common myna has been successfully introduced to eastern Australia, South Africa and various Pacific islands such as Hawaii, Fiji and the Cook group.

Once a pair of common mynas have bred successfully, they usually remain together while they are both alive. They keep a territory for most of the year in which they feed and, in the appropriate season, breed. However, the adults leave the territory each evening to spend the night in a communal roost (except when there are eggs in the nest to incubate). The roost is usually a large tree with dense foliage. At dusk, as hundreds of mynas settle in the roost, their raucous calls are deafening.

Mynas do not have an elaborate musical song like a blackbird, but instead give a rapid sequence of gurgling, whistling, chattering, grating sounds. One common call has been transcribed as *ah-choo-kee, ah-choo-kee.*

Recording: Ngongotaha, February 1957.

KOKAKO
Callaeas cinerea

The kokako, saddleback and huia (extinct) belong together in the New Zealand wattlebird family, which is unique to this country. At the corner of the gape on each side they have a fleshy wattle. Adult kokakos in the North Island have blue wattles and are sometimes called blue-wattled crows. They are as large as crows, but kokakos are not in the crow family, so this name is misleading. South Island kokakos had orange-coloured wattles, but they are now extinct – at least, none has been seen for over forty years.

The kokako is a bird of the tall, dense native bush and sadly it has declined to a few small remnant populations. In the long term it may die out on the mainland and persist only on island sanctuaries like Little Barrier, on which it was recently released. This is all the more sad because the kokako's loud, rich, flute-like song is perhaps the most melodious of all New Zealand birds. The song varies geographically, so over large areas of New Zealand particular songs have gone forever.

'The notes of the male are loud and varied; but the most noticeable one is a long-drawn organ-note of surpassing depth and richness . . . I have often heard two or more kokakos, each in a different key, sounding forth these rich organ-notes with rapturous effect; and it is well worth a night's discomfort in the bush to be awakened at dawn by this rare forest music' (Buller).

Recording: Mapara, near Te Kuiti, January 1988, dawn. (Grey warbler in background.)